The Fifties in Focus

pictures from the Photocentre Collection
Berwick-upon-Tweed

Published by
Berwick-upon-Tweed Record Office
on behalf of
The Friends of Berwick & District Museum and Archives

2016

First published 2016

Copyright: Photographs © Berwick-upon-Tweed Record Office
Text © Friends of Berwick & District Museum and Archives
c/o Berwick-upon-Tweed Record Office,
Walkergate Building,
Walkergate,
Berwick-upon-Tweed
TD15 1DB

ISBN 978 0 9526738 3 5

Printed by:
Martins the Printers,
Sea View Works,
Spittal,
Berwick-upon-Tweed
TD15 1RS

Friends of Berwick & District
Museum and Archives

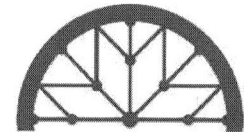

BERWICK-UPON-TWEED
RECORD OFFICE

INTRODUCTION

In September 2012 The Photocentre in Bridge Street, Berwick, closed its doors for the final time. On leaving his post at the Berwick Journal, David Smith started his own press agency in Hide Hill, before moving to 17 Bridge Street in 1953. Over their 60 years in business David Smith, and later his son Ian and their staff photographers, created an archive of well over three million images documenting every aspect of life in Berwick, North Northumberland and the Scottish Borders. To ensure this unique collection stayed in

David Smith

the town, the negatives were purchased by Berwick Record Office with the help of the Friends of Berwick and District Museum and Archives. The images reproduced in this book offer a glimpse of the area between 1951 and 1959 through the lens of David Smith and his staff. It is merely a selection but provides an indication of what has been preserved.

ACKNOWLEDGEMENTS

Thanks are due to the many people who have contributed to this publication, and particularly:

Erica Bamford, Linda Bankier, Jane Bowen, Irene Budworth, Samuel Cole, Lady Rose Crossman, Kevin Graham, Ralph Holmes, Martins the Printers, Carole Pringle, Cameron Robertson, Lars Rose, Wendy Scott, Ellen Smith, John Spiers, Robert Steward, Janet Ward, Jim Waugh.

Front cover: The opening of the May Fair, 1951 (See p. 46)

Back cover: The Photocentre shop window in Bridge Street - BRO 1944/1/1139/2

1952. Wood's hotel on Marygate, established in the late 19th century, was one of Berwick's temperance hotels. It was run by the Wood family, whose best known member was the artist Frank Watson Wood. One of the shops at the front of the hotel was James Bryson, a local bakery and significant local employer.

1953. The Theatre in Hide Hill opened in February 1928 (as Berwick's second cinema/theatre) and it originally offered seating for over 1000 people. It was designed in art-deco style, and the foyer containing the box-office and the sales kiosk was more spacious and modern than that of its rival, The Playhouse, further down the road.

August 1955. This queue at The Theatre was waiting to see the British war film *The Dam Busters*. The Theatre advertised the "Northern premiere" from 25 August and it was then kept on "owing to unprecedented demand". *The Dam Busters* was the most popular film to be shown in British cinemas in 1955.

1955. The Old Bridge Tavern (previously the Old Hen & Chickens Inn) stood in Bridge Street until it was pulled down in 1963 to make way for a car park. During demolition a rare example of 16th century wall painting in tempera on plaster was discovered in an upstairs room. This was restored and is now on display in Berwick Museum.

August 1958. Towers & Bishop was a confectioners and sweet shop on Marygate. It was founded in 1867 by Mr John Bishop, of Dalkeith, and it both manufactured and sold sweets. In 1910, it made and sold Berwick Rangers "clips", a yellow and black boiled sweet flavoured with cinnamon. The shop ceased trading in the 1960s.

Early 1950s. Berwick bus station, with its entrance on Marygate opposite Golden Square, was used by two bus companies in the 1950s, SMT (Scottish Motor Traction) and United Automobile Services. The United bus here on the left is running the mid-morning half-hourly service to Spittal; the SMT bus on the right was bound for Kelso.

BRO 1944/1/518/1

BRO 1944/1/518/4

11 December 1953. The Corn Exchange opened in 1858 and, as well as selling grain, it immediately became a principal venue for many kinds of event in Berwick, including balls, concerts, religious and political meetings, and auctions. The event shown here is the 6th annual grain and root show organised by Berwick and District Young Farmers' Club.

1956. During this drill inspection at the Fire Station in Wallace Green three appliances can be seen: a wartime engine at the back and two Commer engines. Firemen were called out by sirens on the roof of the building. The Wallace Green station, now known as Macdonald House, operated until the 1970s when it moved to Tweedmouth.

June 1953. William Cowe & Son's grocery store in Bridge Street was one of the many shops which were decorated to celebrate the Queen's Coronation. Cowe's was the home of the Original Berwick Cockles, a mint-flavoured sweet made on the premises since 1801. William Cowe bought the shop in 1886 after the death of Robert Weatherhead. It finally closed in 2010.

2 June 1953. Many areas of Berwick put on a Coronation party for children, including this one at Braeside in Prior Park. The children include: Ann Wooley, Alex Spence, Stuart Gregson, Alan, Joan & David Weightman, Marion Crawford, Eileen Newies, Fay Edgeley, Stuart Lyall, Sandy Spence, Kathleen Wooley, Sandra McMenemy. Appalling weather kept most events within tents and caused the cancellation of the promised evening firework display.

7 July 1956. On the Queen's first royal visit to Berwick, she and the Duke of Edinburgh were driven from the station to the newly refurbished Town Hall to meet dignitaries and tour the old gaol. Crowds lined the route, including these at Stoddart's Corner. Stoddart's was a popular provisions shop; to its left stood the Salmon Hotel.

7 July 1956. One of the best positions for seeing the arrival of the Queen was at the corner of Eastern Lane and Marygate, outside Lee's (jewellers and watchmakers). The onlookers include: Olive Wilkinson, Margaret Pierpoint, Kathleen Hope, Ethel Purvis, Annie Johnson, Margaret Glenton, and Dorothy Paterson.

7 July 1956. In Tweedmouth below the Royal Tweed Bridge, the Queen and Duke of Edinburgh met nine foremen fishermen to hear about the salmon trade. A 12 pound salmon, freshly caught at Low Bells fishery, was presented to the monarch by Tom Elliot, a lifelong salmon fisherman (who was also interviewed by Richard Dimbleby in his 1950 film about Berwick).

29 June 1958. When the Queen and Duke of Edinburgh came to Holy Island - said to be the first visit by a reigning monarch since Saxon times - an estimated 9000 people gathered, including these well-wishers in Market Place. The visit included the Lifeboat station, the parish church, and a meeting with island fishermen.

29 June 1958. Crowds waved the Queen farewell from the Lifeboat Station on Holy Island. After her visit the Queen departed by launch, taking her back to the Royal Yacht Britannia which was moored offshore but concealed in a heavy sea-mist. There she hosted a luncheon.

25 July 1957. The Duchess of Kent, as President of the Royal National Lifeboat Association, visited Spittal for the launch of Berwick's new lifeboat, the *William and Mary Durham*. In this picture, on Dock Road, she was welcomed by the Mayor, Captain Tom Evans.

25 July 1957. The *William and Mary Durham* lifeboat was constructed using oak and mahogany. Length: 42 ft; beam 12 ft; draught 3 ft 7 in. Its top speed was 8 knots. Its range was 235 nautical miles. It had a crew of 8, and it could carry up to 70 people in rough weather, or 100 in normal conditions.

1952. Berwick quayside is seen here soon after shipbuilding was resumed on the site. On the right, steel sheets for ship hulls can be seen, held in place by 'kickers'. The stores at the back left have now disappeared, but the square building in the centre still stands. At back right, the Playhouse cinema (now demolished) is partially visible.

1952. Berwick shipyard's slipway is shown here in the centre with boats under construction on either side. As well as the slipway, boats would sometimes be launched sideways. The shipyard was a major employer in the town until it closed in 1979.

16 May 1951. The *Naughton* was an 80 ton motor barge, and the first welded steel ship to be built in Berwick. It was built by William Weatherhead & Sons of Cockenzie, who in 1950 set up their shipyard on Berwick quayside, where Berwick shipbuilding had first been established in the 18th century. Here it is being launched down the slipway by Mrs D. S. Clarabut.

1956. Sometimes a boat had to leave Berwick shipyard by road rather than water, and taking it through the town's narrow streets was a challenging operation. This motor launch is being eased around Bridge End on a trailer. In the left foreground, the man carrying a camera is Alex West, photographer for the *Berwick Advertiser*.

1952. William Leith's, sailmakers, occupied a former maltings building on Pier Road (today converted into flats), where they utilised the extensive floorspace and heavy beams necessary for handling large pieces of canvas and tarpaulin. Sewing machines are on the right. The manufacture of tents and marquees, seen here, became their main activity.

1958. The Lee family of Tweedmouth built boats at their yard in Dock Road for nearly two centuries. The picture shows one of their cobles, made for the Berwick Salmon Company, being loaded on to a lorry. The railway embankment to the right of the road has since been removed. Lees Lane in Tweedmouth is named after the family.

1952. A net for the salmon fishing is being made at the Carr Rock. The net is being sewn to the float rope; cork floats from Portugal were used. On the right stood the old fishing shiel.

1952. Crabwater, by Berwick pier, was unusual in being a fishery that rowed 'southwards' (catching the fish moving downstream). At the far end of the pier stands the harbour master's house. The building to the left was a seated shelter with toilets, while above it stood the coastguard station.

1952. These boxes of Tweed salmon have arrived at the railway station for onward transport. Numbered boxes were used which were returnable on deposit. Usually everything was sent by rail but sometimes, when there were too many boxes, transport by lorry would be used, as seen here.

February 1955. Ralph Holmes & Sons had been fish & game dealers in Berwick since 1853, with shops in Bridge Street and Church Street. This mobile refrigerated fish shop, apparently the first of its kind in the country, started work in February around North Northumberland and the Borders. It was fitted out to allow the customers to enter the van and shop in comfort, whatever the weather.

BRO 1944/1/1899/14

25 March 1958. Seven Massey Ferguson 35 tractors are seen here lined up outside the premises of William Elder & Sons in Castlegate. The man on the extreme right is Jardine Elder. The firm had been ironfounders and manufacturers of agricultural equipment since the mid-19th century, and they moved from Tweedmouth to these larger premises in 1907.

December 1959. A wide range of William Elder's stock can be seen here in the showroom, from tractors (2 Massey Ferguson 35s/3 Massey Ferguson 65s and a Massey Ferguson TE20) to feed troughs, rolls of wire fencing, (foreground) silage harvester. At the back of the showroom was a series of offices. The showroom had its front window on Castlegate (photographer has his back to it).

December 1959. William Elder's fitting shop is a hive of activity. The man in the centre is bending the tin for a double sheep/cattle feeding trough. The man drilling holes to his left was called Albert and his job was just to drill holes. The trailer to the front right is the base for a turnip cutter. These would be drawn behind a tractor.

1956. James Pringle, the knitwear firm, opened a branch in Berwick in February 1948 (among the first on the Tweedside Industrial Estate), and it expanded to become one of the town's largest employers. It provided important job opportunities for women especially, needing skilled intarsia knitters. Its closure in the 1990s was a major blow to Berwick's economy.

23 May 1954. En route for Scotland, the circus owner Billy Smart led a procession of 10 elephants from Berwick station to the Scottish Border, accompanied by nearly 150 local children. At Lamberton Toll they were greeted by pipers and the Mayor of Berwick, Alderman G. M. Lamb. The elephant procession then returned to Berwick to reboard the train for Edinburgh.

1954. Before the opening of the A1 bypass, all north- and south-bound road traffic had to pass through the centre of Berwick. This 125-foot crane girder blocks Marygate while careful manoeuvring is conducted to take it around Stoddart's Corner. Marygate was still cobbled at this date.

22 August 1954. The opening ceremony of the Holy Island causeway took place on a stormy August afternoon. About 200 people assembled to see the Duchess of Northumberland cut the ribbon to open the first road link to Holy Island, but most were unable to hear anything above the roar of the wind as it whistled over the sand.

22 August 1954. The Duchess of Northumberland travelled in this van followed by another 50 vehicles across the newly opened Holy Island causeway. As her vehicle crossed the bridge, the Island women sang "Keep right on to the end of the road". In the background are the famous Holy Island taxis which went through the water and knew the safe route along the sands.

BRO 1944/1/55/12

21 August 1952. 17 buses were lined up in Marygate for the annual outing of the Berwick & District Old Age Pensioners Association. Over 500 pensioners were given a civic send-off as they departed on a trip through the Borders. They included 95-year-old George Urquhart and 92-year-old Margaret Younger.

BRO 1944/1/55/11

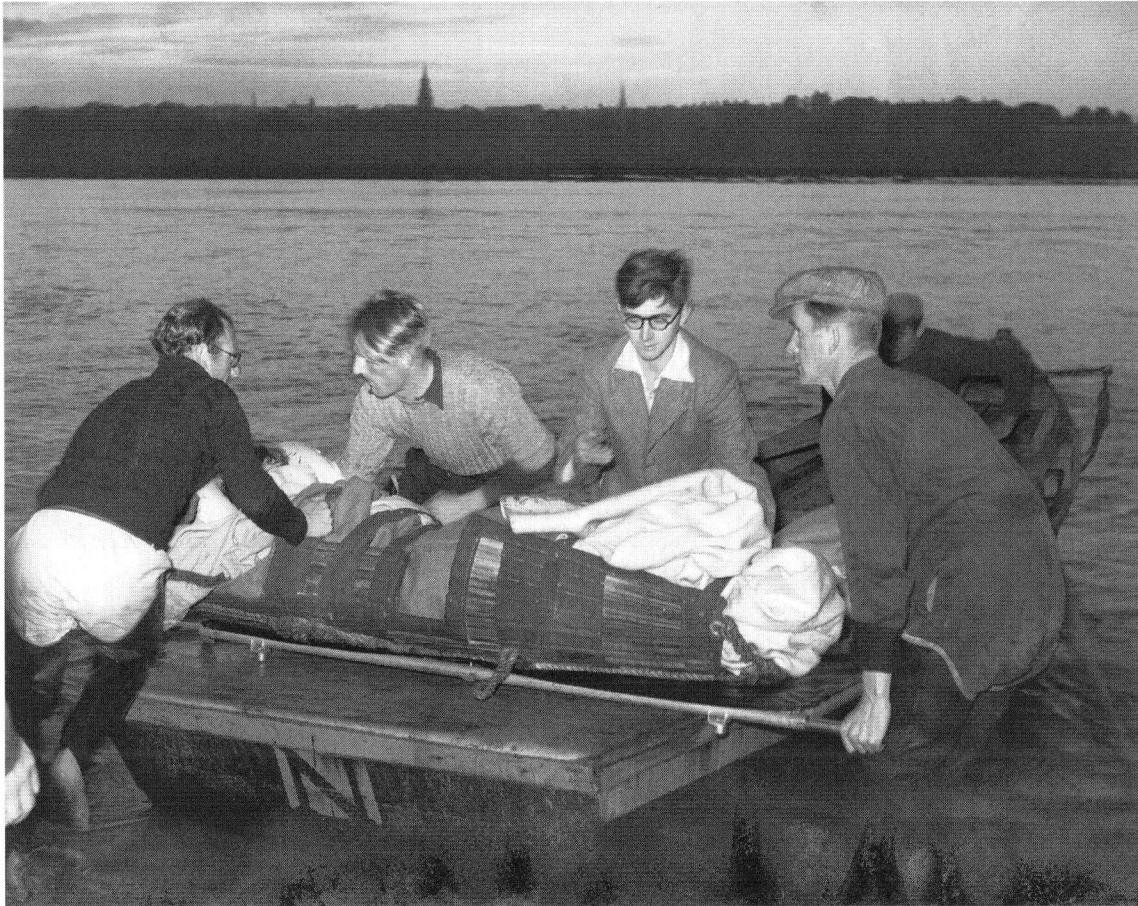

25 June 1952. Two airmen were rescued from the North Sea when a Shackleton bomber exploded and crashed while on a naval exercise. The two survivors were brought ashore in Berwick by the Holy Island lifeboat; at Carr Rock they were transferred to salmon cobles to be rowed to a waiting ambulance.

BRO 1944/1/519/2

28 October 1953. There was a miraculous escape for the 65 passengers on board the overnight Glasgow-Colchester train when it came off the rails at Goswick at 1.00 a.m. The locomotive ploughed on for more than 100 yards ripping up rails and sleepers before landing on its side. Only one person, a man from Berwick, suffered slight injury (in contrast to the more serious Goswick rail crash of 1947).

20 September 1955. In the early hours of the morning, a lorry loaded with fruit crashed into a house at Railway Cottages on Prince Edward Road in Tweedmouth. Despite the damage, the driver and passenger were only slightly injured. Hundreds of oranges were scattered around the area, to the delight of local children.

1952. Berwick Barracks served as the regimental headquarters of the King's Own Scottish Borderers from 1881 to 1963. New recruits would come there for their training. The officers' mess can be seen at the back right of the Barracks square.

BRO 1944/1/71/1

22 September 1951. On this date the last Quarter Sessions Court was held in Berwick Town Hall. It ended a 400 year tradition of hearing serious criminal cases in the town including those carrying the death sentence. This privilege was granted under its royal charters. Here the Recorder is inspecting the stocks, sited on the opposite side of the building to today.

1 May 1952. On Thursday morning 17 riders gathered on the Parade to ride the Bounds. They were led off by Jack Moffat of Bowsden, on his 43rd consecutive ride. Councillor Lamb also accompanied them, the first Mayor to take part on horseback for over 100 years. In the background are the army huts which were home to National Service soldiers.

1 May 1957. Mr John Moffat of Holborn led off the riders from the Parade. He first rode the Bounds when he was 5 and this was said to be his 50th consecutive ride. 20 riders set off, 15 of whom were female. The youngest was Margaret Hill of Prior Hill in Tweedmouth.

25 May 1951. The crowds are gathered here before the Town Hall steps to hear Mr Davison, Town Clerk, read the ancient proclamation opening the May Fair. The fair was described as one of the biggest and busiest since 1939 with 34 stalls set out along Marygate. These included stalls for linoleum, china and clothes. The traffic struggled to travel along the street.

25 May 1956. On a sunny day, The Mayor, Alderman Mrs B. F. C. Adams, and the Sheriff, William Elder, continued a centuries' old tradition of officially opening Berwick May Fair by "Walking the Fair". They processed up Marygate past all the stalls, accompanied by the Civic Party of councillors and town officials, including Mr Davison, the Town Clerk.

BRO 1944/1/670/1

22 July 1954. The crowning of the Salmon Queen traditionally took place in mid-July as part of the celebrations for the Tweedmouth Feast during the Berwick Trades Fortnight's Holiday. In 1954 the queen was Maude Grey, with attendants Daphne Martin & Marie Peacock, trainbearers Betty Price & Pamela Rosie, escorted by the Berwick Sea Rovers.

16 July 1959. The Salmon Queen being crowned in 1959 was Valerie Campbell, with attendants Sally Hewson & Elizabeth Patterson and trainbearers Wendy Burgon & Patricia Shiel. The event was one of the annual occasions when the 'shows' came to town and set up their attractions between the New Bridge and West End Green (now divided by new housing).

23 July 1953. As part of the annual celebrations for the Tweedmouth Feast, a carnival procession made a tour of Berwick, Tweedmouth and Spittal. The interpretation of "Dixieland" for this Woolworth's float might cause offence now, but in its day it won second prize for best float in the competition.

1951. Berwick Amateur Rowing Club. *Back row, left to right:* Eric Black, Gerald Bryson, Ken Thompson, Alex Gilchrist, Gerald Heslop, Ian Turner. *Middle:* Alex Burgon (boatman), Jim Matthewson, Barty Lough, Allan Taylor, Jimmy Wood, Les Ellison, Adam Middlemiss, Dick Brown, Jimmy Cromarty, Alf Morgan (boatman). *Front:* Robert Grieve, Jim Renton, Tom Fairbairn, George Payne, Jimmy Smith, Jim Payne, Charlie Inkpen. *Coxes:* Lawton, Taylor.

1952. Turf is being laid for a new football pitch at Shielfield. Berwick Rangers leased 6 acres of land in 1951 to create a new stadium adjacent to their old pitch, but funds were scarce. Turf was taken from the surrounding area of the old pitch and local farmers and gardeners were asked to contribute any turf they could spare.

February 1951. Berwick Rangers supporters are seen heading off by train to a Scottish Cup match against Brechin City. About 500 people travelled by train from Berwick, many of them wearing Rangers' rosettes, hats and scarves. Brechin won 3 - 2. In 1951 Rangers were admitted to the precursor of the Scottish Football League, in which they have played ever since.

1952. Until the opening of a pool at the Corn Exchange in 1972, Berwick had only outdoor swimming pools. At the Greenses beach, there were separate Gentlemen's and Ladies' pools, the remains of which can still be seen.

June 1957. Here, the signal has just been given for the release of thousands of racing pigeons on the trackside at Berwick Station. The birds were taking part in a national race sponsored by *The People* newspaper. They were brought by train and unloaded in their baskets by local fanciers who also helped with the liberation.

BRO 1944/1/2/4

1951. This Vauxhall Velox was driven in the Monte Carlo Rally in January 1951 by Jack Stoddart, of Berwick, and A. H. M. Edney, of Newcastle. The two men completed the arduous journey from Glasgow to Monte Carlo and came 42nd in the time trials. The car was serviced at Blackburn & Price's garage, established in 1946 in Palace Green in Berwick; the auto electrician (*left*) was Ernie Hope.

1 December 1954. The British racing driver Mike Hawthorn was guest of honour at Berwick Motor Club's annual dinner and prize-giving at the Rum Puncheon. *Left to right:* T. A. Irvine, Newcastle, winner of the Border Rally; Mike Hawthorn; A. M. Calder; Jack Stoddart, winner of the Attendance Cup.

1956. For the Monte Carlo Rally of 1956, the Stoddart brothers, Jack and William, competed with their Standard Vanguard No 214. They completed the course and came in with a final position of 159th. This picture shows them with their vehicle in the Golden Square garage.

BRO 1944/1/1939/9

1958. The racetrack at Charterhall, on a former RAF airfield near Greenlaw in Berwickshire, was established in 1952, and Jim Clark won his first important race here in 1957. Jim Clark (*centre*) is seen here with a D Type Jaguar, which he drove in some 20 races that season, winning 12 of them.

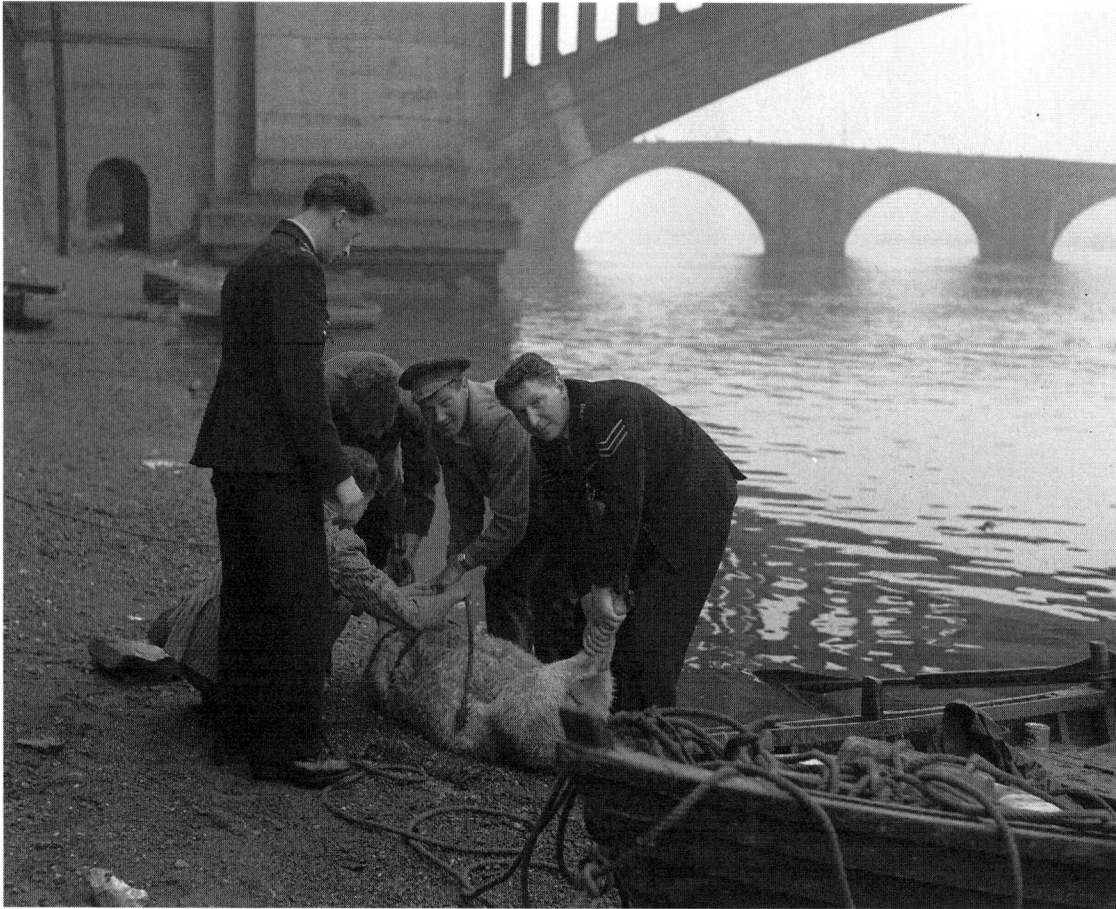

BRO 1944/1/994/1

22 August 1955. Five men and two salmon cobles were employed in the recapture of a sheep which leapt over the parapet of Berwick's Old Bridge into the River Tweed. It was being driven to the slaughterhouse in Tweedmouth when it broke loose and made a bid for freedom. After half an hour the sheep was lassoed and towed ashore, and then sent to its original destination.

An index to the black and white photographs in the Photocentre Collection, including their reference numbers, is available on the website of The Friends of Berwick & District Museum and Archives:

www.berwickfriends.org.uk/record-office/catalogues/

The index is regularly updated. The photographs cover North Northumberland and the Scottish Borders. They include local events and shows, weddings and buildings.

Requests for copies of photographs should be addressed to:

Berwick-upon-Tweed Record Office,
Walkergate Building,
Walkergate,
Berwick-upon-Tweed
TD15 1DB

Email: berwickarchives@woodhorn.org.uk